KT-498-501

SO NOW THEN

SHELBY LEE ADAMS

ADAM BROOMBERG AND OLIVER CHANARIN

CHIEN-CHI CHANG

JULIO GRINBLATT

AN-MY LÊ

SUSAN MEISELAS

BORIS MIKHAILOV

SIMON NORFOLK

TRENT PARKE

WENG PEIJUN

PAUL SHAMBROOM

MASSIMO VITALI

MICHAEL WESELY

SO NOW THEN

EDITED BY CHRISTOPHER COPPOCK & PAUL SEAWRIGHT

ESSAYS BY DAVID CAMPANY, MARTHA LANGFORD & JAN-ERIK LUNDSTRÖM

SO NOW THEN
Published by Ffotogallery, Cardiff
in association with the Hereford Photography Festival 2006
www.photofest.org

FFOTOGALLERY
c/o Chapter Arts Centre, Market Road, Cardiff CF5 1QE, www.ffotogallery.org
Ffotogallery is supported by the Arts Council of Wales & Cardiff County Council

Publication design: Tony Waddingham/Oblique

Publication editing: Christopher Coppock & Paul Seawright

Publication production: Christopher Coppock & Tony Waddingham

Copy proofing: Lis Edwards

Front cover: Weng Peijun, *Bird's Eye View – Shanghai*, 2002

Cover printed on Magno Star 135 g/m^2

Text printed on Arctic the Volume 150 g/m^2

Printed by Antilope Printing, Industriestraat 5, I.Z. Hagenbroek, 2500 Lier, Belgium

ISBN-10: 1 872771 65 3

ISBN-13: 978 1 872771 65 6

Published June 2006

Photographs © The Photographers

© Ffotogallery Wales Limited 2006

Texts © David Campany, Martha Langford & Jan-Erik Lundström, 2006

Chien-Chi Chang, Susan Meiselas & Trent Parke are represented by Magnam Photos

So Now Then was commissioned by Hereford Photography Festival and launched at Hay Festival 2006, Hay-on-Wye, Wales

INTRODUCTION

The Hereford Photography Festival is the only annual festival of photography in Britain, and for fifteen years has mounted an enterprising and ambitious exhibition programme in the rural city of Hereford. The festival has consistently privileged documentary practice and this major publication seeks to address recent developments within that context. In an attempt to represent a spectrum of conceptual and aesthetic opinion about the current status of documentary, we drew up an international list of over sixty seminal figures, writers, critics, educationalists and curators, asking them to nominate one photographer who they felt was significantly contributing to, and developing, the documentary debate (consciously or unconsciously). The invitation emphasized our understanding of the term as broadly catholic, and our motivation was to assemble a shortlist of photographers and artists who were pushing subject boundaries – or were innovating, methodologically or critically. Although a number of the names that surfaced were predictably conservative, the majority were practitioners who have extended established conventions. From the outset, we were aware that the emergent selection could never be comprehensive, neither would it necessarily echo what we might have independently chosen (we longed for some names to come forward that didn't), but we believe these eloquent bodies of work do begin to suggest a frisson within the genre at this particular time.

Documentary practice has had a difficult time since the 1960s, suffering a crisis of confidence in the post-structuralist-dominated 1980s and vying for legitimacy, after decades that saw it defined as an uncritical and pseudo-humanist pursuit. Documentary found itself thrust into debates surrounding new thinking about representation – inevitable really given its inexorable relationship with the real – and photographers who were committed to a critical practice began to question the medium's usefulness in this context. In particular, a number of British photographers working in the mid 1980s began to make work that challenged long-established views of actuality, objectivity and the photographer's role as innocent bystander. Subsequently subjectivity became the touchstone of the 1990s, reaching its peak in the confessional work of Nan Goldin, Richard Billingham and Gillian Wearing at the end of the decade. Paul Graham's seminal series from Northern Ireland, *Troubled Land*, Martin Parr's *Last Resort* and Chris Killip and Graham Smith's *Another Country* were deliberately conscious of the authorial voice, but perhaps more significantly left a trace of narrative rebelliousness that runs though much of the work in this book. In this sense, the dismantling of some of the central tenets of documentary is perhaps complete. For the most part, the thirteen bodies of work presented here do not rely on associated text, do not insist on anchored narrative and often draw their success from a fluidity of meaning, refusing passive reading, pressing us to revisit pictures and unravel intention and nuance.

While other dominant photographic genres, portraiture, landscape, staged photography, have slipped effortlessly into the vocabulary of contemporary art practice, documentary has struggled for acceptance, until more recently. Photojournalism, hovering on the periphery of documentary practice, has remained relatively unreconstructed. It isn't uncommon, even now, to hear photojournalists cast themselves in the classic paternalistic role of benign witnesses to global events. An-My Lê, Luc Delahaye, Chien-Chi Chang, Susan Meiselas, eloquently demonstrate how photographers can comfortably share the subject matter of the photojournalist whilst adopting the more sophisticated and mass-market-free vocabulary of the artist, avoiding the synoptic reductionism of much of the editorial world.

Given the seismic shifts in the political landscape since September 11th 2001, there is an increased urgency and indeed immediacy in how we consume news imagery since the defining televisual experience of the terrorist attacks on New York. As people generally are bombarded visually by politics and international affairs, it becomes critical that artists lend their voices to debates traditionally dominated by global media agencies – debates at the heart of documentary practice. This isn't entirely new: video artists like

Mark Wallinger, Willie Doherty and Shirin Neshat have been engaging the socio-political subject of the documentarist for some time, but would never refer to themselves as such – nor would many of those included in this publication.

Since *Documenta 11*, the subject of documentary has taken on a new mantle within the contemporary art world, where the genre, once disparaged, has been afforded a fresh, chic status. Subsequently, Tate Modern's *Cruel and Tender* 'blockbuster' foregrounded a number of mainstream photographers central to an understanding of contemporary documentary practice – Paul Graham, Martin Parr, Michael Schmidt, Reneke Dijkstra – and the following year curated a major Robert Frank retrospective. Tate Liverpool's 2006 exhibition *Making History: Art and Documentary in Britain from 1929 to Now*, in their own words, focused on works where a dialogue between art and realist documentary occurs and set out to question the traditional demarcation between art and documentary, and to ask whether this is really a false dichotomy. Whether these institutions are adopting these new curatorial strategies to embed the art of photography in contemporary visual art remains to be seen. Nonetheless, such mainstream contexts do create prominent opportunities for photographers making important work about issues that define our past and shape our future.

We are indebted to the writers, David Campany (UK), Martha Langford (Canada) and Jan-Erik Lundström (Sweden), who have contributed three imaginative essays to the book: texts which tease out, in very distinct ways, the many debates that circumscribe the rich terrain that constitutes documentary practice as – we think – we know it.

This book is about now, the present, not just in photographic terms, but where we find ourselves as an evolving global community. It is no coincidence that a third of the work here is concerned with conflict and other series trawl profound subjects like the industrial revolution engulfing China, the rebuilding of East Berlin, disintegration of society in post-Soviet Ukraine, home-made bombs mimicking everyday objects in the Middle East and incisive glimpses of the everyday; life in the isolated Appalachians, birthday and holiday rituals, the streets of Sydney, the machinations of local government. Whatever the semantics – social documentary/realism/political art, the work in this book remains urgent and critically important, so, now, and even then…

Christopher Coppock
Director, Ffotogallery
The National Development Agency for Photography in Wales

Paul Seawright
Dean, Newport School of Art Media & Design
University of Wales, Newport

STRAIGHT PICTURES OF A CROOKED WORLD

DAVID CAMPANY

fig. 1

This book is a survey of documentary photography in current art. Documentary has had a place in art and art has had a place in documentary. This has always been so, although the nature of the relation changes. The recent rise of art in contemporary culture, for example, has meant that documentary has found a new profile in the gallery system. It has also found itself aestheticized, sometimes over-aestheticized, in its more traditional outlets. This has consequences, not just for documentary practice itself, but for the way it is thought about, written about and debated. These days art does have a way of regarding itself as the privileged arena for the discussion of documentary photography (indeed, for the discussion of nearly all types of photography). Or, to put it another way, questions of aesthetics and the predilections of an often fickle art culture have come to dominate discussions of documentary like never before.

When documentary photography is critically discussed the focus tends to be on the practices that have a currency in art. This may be understandable and even helpful, but it is also odd. It is like studying a tiger in a zoo, not in the wild. Documentary behaves differently in art and so do its audiences. Some have suggested, a little rashly, that documentary no longer exists in the wild – that it is an endangered species, surviving only in protected environments, such as art. So quick to announce the end of everything but itself, art sometimes fails to see beyond its own outlook.

One of the paradoxes of documentary photography is that while it has been central to the description of the present and the construction of history, it has made its impact in forms that are transient and ephemeral. Magazines and newspapers are especially so. Photographs themselves may live on in other contexts. Art history is slightly more robust than documentary history and it tells its own version of documentary's past and present. Firstly, it tends to privilege those documentarists who were or are sceptical of many of documentary's claims. Think of Bill Brandt, Henri Cartier-Bresson or Walker Evans. ('Documentary?' Evans puzzled, toward the end of his life, 'That's a very sophisticated and misleading word. And not really clear… The term should be *documentary style*… You see, a document has use, whereas art is really useless. Therefore art is never a document, though it certainly can adopt that style.') Secondly, documentary photography evolved in a close and complex relation with journalism. Few documentarists are naive enough to assume that photographs work alone. However, the artistic ambition of photographers and curators has been, in the main, to tear photographs out of journalism. Of course it is not that once in art, photographs function as purely visual statements. Journalism is still necessary but it slips into other guises – art theory and criticism, the catalogue essay, the promotional blurb, the review, the visually withheld conceptual 'key' to the work, and so forth. Thirdly, and this is the most pertinent point to make here, 'para-documentary' forms take root within art. This is the most appropriate way to think of the projects gathered in this book. A few are made by photographers who also operate outside of art (Adam Broomberg and Oliver Chanarin, for example). Most are not.

A couple of years ago I wrote an essay on photography in contemporary art. In it I pointed out that:

> in art we see what we might call the art concept of the fashion image; of the snapshot; of the portrait; of the medical photograph, the architectural photograph; the film still; the passport photo; the archival image; the penal image; of kitsch; of the topographic image; of the documentary image and so on.

It seemed to me that:

> the gallery has become the space to look askew at the general field of the photographic, to engage directly or indirectly with a commentary upon the image world at large. The space of art has thus come to function either as a dissecting table to which the different forms of the photographic are brought for creative reflection, or as a set upon which they can be can be reworked. These two metaphors – dissecting table

fig. 2

fig. 3

fig. 4

and set – map quite well on to what seem to be the two key impulses behind much current photographic art: the forensic interest in detail and the cinematic interest in mise-en-scène or staging. These impulses are so forcefully present today because all photography in art is somehow obliged to enter into a dialogue either with the notion of the photo as visual evidence or with the culture of the moving image in which the still now finds itself. Or both.[1]

I found myself returning to this assessment when looking at a retrospective in London of the art photographer Jeff Wall. Wall currently classifies his images broadly in two categories: 'documentary' or 'cinematographic'. His *catalogue raisonné* defines the terms:

> The term 'documentary' applies to those photographs in which the artist chooses the location and time of the picture but without any kind of intervention on his part. The use of this term is consistent with the normative meaning of the term 'documentary photography'.

and,

> The term cinematographic applies to those photographs in which the subject of the picture has been prepared in some way, ranging from minimal modifications to the construction of entire sets, creation of costumes and objects etc.[2]

So for example his *Clipped Branches, East Cordova St., Vancouver* (1999; fig. 1) is a documentary photograph, presumably because the branches were not clipped by Wall, nor *for* his photograph. His photographic labour is separate from the world's labour. The former records the latter. *A Woman with a Covered Tray* (2003; fig. 2) is defined as cinematographic, presumably because the woman carries the tray for Wall's photograph (even though she might be pretending not to). Here Wall labours as a photographer and as a director. This is all he means by the 'cinematographic' photograph. The image is made by way of pre-paration and collaboration – it need not look like cinema – and it suspends documentary's traditional assertions.

This binary scheme is simple and useful. And, like any simple scheme, it is most useful when it breaks down. Let us consider a range of documentary projects that have been visible in art of late. Adam Broomberg and Oliver Chanarin have photographed *Chicago* (2005–6). They describe it thus: 'Hidden from view by the topography of the Negev desert, Chicago is a mock-up Arab town built by the Israeli Defense Force for training in urban combat.' They have also photographed thin strips of tree plantation in Israel that are strategically placed to suggest Israel has 'made the whole desert bloom'. Chris Stewart has photographed *Kill House* (2005; fig. 3), '…a house in Arkansas, USA, that was built for the purpose of training private military personnel to clear domestic houses in conflict zones such as Iraq and Afghanistan'. An-My Lê's extensive project *Small Wars* (2005) includes images of Vietnam War re-enactments and US military training exercises for future action in the Gulf. Sarah Pickering's *Public Order* (2004; fig. 4) is a suite of photographs that document 'the ambiguous urban landscape of the UK's Metropolitan Police Public Order Training Centre, an unreal constructed world of civic intransigence and imagined threat'. Larry Sultan's *The Valley* (2002) documents the boredom and fakery at the heart of the making of porn films in Los Angeles. Stefan Ruiz's *Factory of Dreams* (2004; fig. 5) looks at the sets and actors of Mexican television soap opera. Seung Woo Back's *Real World* (2004; fig. 6) documents a theme park in Seoul that gathers scaled-down versions of the world's architectural landmarks. Steffi Klenz's *Nonsuch* (2005) is a cool study of Poundbury, the 'traditional' English town built in Dorset in the late 1980s according to the 'social philosophy' of Prince Charles.

What do these projects have in common? Firstly, there is artifice in all this work, but it is not essentially of the photographers' making. Artifice is their subject matter. If the projects are documentary, it is in the sense that there is a division between the photographers' activities and the situations they photograph. There is also a common visual style to this work. The photographers generally use the camera in ways familiar

fig. 5   fig. 6

to the nineteenth century. Their procedure is slow, deliberating and involves large film-formats and tripods. The photography is formal, rectilinear and in deep focus. The distances between the camera and the subject are kept fairly consistent across each project, as is the light. This is to say that most of these photographers opt for the 'straight' photograph handed down from traditional architectural and topographic photography, via the work of Walker Evans and August Sander, and secured in art via Bernd and Hilla Becher, Lewis Baltz and Robert Adams.

In these works documentary forgoes its traditional recording of 'events', preferring to focus on preparation for them.[3] Rather than grounding a concrete reality, the extreme objectivity of these photographs has an unexpected, inverse effect. They flip us into the register of hyper-real simulation of the kind we associate with the aesthetics of 'virtual reality'. It is no coincidence these photographers adopt the forced monocular perspectives typical of video-game graphics, with their surveying 'point of view' shots. Moreover, they share something of the video game's status as model, as fantasy of worldly control, as safe rehearsal in an arena of imaginary mastery.

Current as it is, this kind of approach does have a history. In 1946 the modernist art critic Clement Greenberg reviewed a show of photographs by Edward Weston. Greenberg wrote little on photography – his famous commitment to 'medium specificity' was concerned in the main with painting. For him painting's subject should be the paint, the canvas and the surface. That way, the medium could achieve a self-reflexivity. By contrast photography is inherently descriptive, and Greenberg suggested that is what it should do. It should describe the world in detail, even though that is not a very reflexive act. However, he singled out for special attention the photographs Weston had made in 1939 (fig. 7) on the back-lots of MGM film studios in Hollywood:

> the best pictures in Weston's show are two frontal views of 'ghost sets' in a movie studio. Here the camera's sharply focused eye is unable to replace the details left out

by the scene painter or architect; and the smoothly painted surfaces prevent the eye from discovering details it would inevitably find in nature or the weathered surface of a real house. At the same time a certain decorative unity is given in advance by the unity, such as it is, of the stage set.[4]

It is easy to see why Greenberg was drawn to these photographs. This is realist photography turned in on itself, in a kind of *trompe l'oeil*. It is photography about the world but also about representation, *en abyme*. In Weston's work and in the other projects I describe here, it seems that two conflicting demands are satisfied. The photographs describe the surface of the world. In this they appear whole, integral, unified, even pictorial. At the same time they are also fragmentary, metaphorical, allegorical, appropriationist, quotational, dissimulationist and intertextual. A loop is made between a modernist idea of photography being 'true' to its descriptive capacities, and the more postmodern demand for a reflexive account of the photograph as a complex social document.

There seems little doubt now that photography really is good at describing the surface appearance of things. That is certainly what these works do. The problems of representation, which are often assumed to stem from the camera, are here displaced on to the world. These images seem less to do with whether photography is an adequate means of representing the world and more to do with whether the world can represent itself. Photography aspires here to be an honest record of worldly deception. Photography is not the trap – the world is the trap. Or, more accurately, photography has so permeated the world that at times we cannot see it as anything more than a re- or pre-presentation.

This kind of strategy seems to satisfy several of art's current demands of documentary photography. Overt 'creativity' is minimized, resulting in images that appear 'cool' and 'level-headed'. It is serial and hence 'reliable', which satisfies publishers as much as curators and critics. It is 'conceptually' driven, i.e. we can 'see' the visual strategy at work quite clearly. And the general sense of restraint in such work courts ambiguity.

fig. 7

(fig.1) Clipped Branches, East Cordova St., Vancouver, 1999 © Jeff Wall. Courtesy Galerie Rüdiger Schöttle, Munich

(fig.2) A Woman with a Covered Tray, 2003 © Jeff Wall. Courtesy Galerie Rüdiger Schöttle, Munich

(fig.3) Kill House, Arkansas, USA, 2005 © Christopher Stewart

(fig.4) High Street, Barricade, 2002, from the 'Public Order' series (2002–5) © Sarah Pickering

(fig.5) Televisa's Studio 9: the central set from Amarte es mi pecado (Loving You is My Sin), 2003 © Stefan Ruiz. Courtesy Impressions Gallery

(fig.6) Real World © Seung Woo Back

(fig.7) MGM Studios 1939. Photograph by Edward Weston. Collection Center for Creative Photography © 1981 Arizona Board of Regents

There are risks in pursuing documentary ambiguity so doggedly. For example, while this work might make an ethical call for our critical engagement with the world and its representation, that call is deliberately muted. It can easily be ignored in preference for a languishing in ambiguity for its own lofty but potentially conservative ends. More to the point, this kind of ambiguity is largely a matter of context. These works adopt the look of the functional document to such an extent that they are often indistinguishable from the kinds of image these institutions make of *themselves*. Pick up a brochure or visit any website for military training facilities, war re-enactment groups or theme parks and see for yourself. The only real difference is art's preference for detail, formal restraint and 'uncanny emptiness' (i.e. they have fewer people in them).

Looking again at this loose list of projects, I see that they fall into two groups. Half are concerned with the military and related institutions of the state. The other half are concerned with the leisure industry – cinema, television, porn, theme parks and so on. Do they have something in common? Why do they attract photographers and why do they shoot them in this way, as straight pictures of a crooked world? Put simply, it strikes me that the war industry and leisure industry are concrete realities that continue to shape our world. They are also primary sources of the fantasies that shape our world.

Notes

1   David Campany, 'On Thinking and not Thinking Photography', *Engage*, 14 (2004).

2   Jeff Wall, *Catalogue Raisonné*, 1978–2004 (Steidl / Schaulager).

3   Elsewhere I have discussed another form of documentary photography's displacement from the event. The 'late photograph' is made as a memorial revisit to the site of the event. We can see the work of Simon Norfolk, included in this book, as an instance of this. See David Campany, 'Safety in Numbness. Some remarks on problems of "Late Photography"', in Green and Lowry (eds), *Where is the Photograph?* (Photoforum / Photoworks, 2003).

4   Clement Greenberg, 'The Camera's Glass Eye: a review of an exhibition of Edward Weston', *Nation*, 9 March 1946. Reprinted in David Campany (ed.), *Art and Photography* (Phaidon, 2003).

AN-MY LÊ

Representations of war and the spectacle of the battleground are central to the work of An-My Lê. She has produced a number of poignant photographic tableaux working with Vietnam War re-enacters and, more recently, has photographed US military exercises in the American desert in preparation for war in Iraq and Afghanistan. These large-format works from the series *29 Palms* allow us not only to – literally – experience the theatre of war but also to deliberate on how the landscape becomes subjugated to the military machine. Heavily informed by current debates about documentary and staged photography, the work is pictorially astute and conceptually rigorous.

Colonel Greenwood, 2003–4

Bivouac, 2003–4

Infantry Platoon, 2003–4

Resupply Operations, 2003–4

Mortar Impact, 2003–4

Mechanized Assault, 2003–4

LCAC (Landing Craft Air-Cushioned), 2003–4

PAUL SHAMBROOM

Lewiston, Minnesota [Population 1,484]
City Council, March 10 1999
Roger Laufenburger, Denny Engrav, Gary Sauers & Rob Rys (City Administrator)

Meetings, a series of apparently innocuous observations of local council meetings in American towns – produced by the photographer between 1999 and 2003 – represents an attempt to understand and illuminate seemingly overwhelming and abstract power-systems. Although town council and community meetings are effectively open to the public, the process of governance remains almost opaque and separate from the lives of ordinary people. The photographs flag up the theatricality and formalism of these democratic forums, which represent an important part of the decision-making process directly affecting the lives of small communities across America.

Wayne County, Utah [Population 2,114]
Board of Commissioners, April 5 1999
Scott Durfey, Clenn Okerlund & Stan Allen

Carefree, Arizona [Population 2,927]
Common Council, April 6 1999
Greg Gardner, Wayne Fischer, Hugh Stevens (Mayor), Julian Barrozala, (Vice Mayor), Edward Morgan & Donald Synder

Dobbins Heights, North Carolina [Population 936]
Town Council, November 8 2001
Mary Magee (Clerk), Channie McManus, Nell Moody, Christine Davis & Gracie Jackson (Mayor Pro Tem)

M M. WARD, SR.
Mayor

CHRISTINE G. DAVIS
COUNCILPERSON

GRACIE C. JACKSON
Mayor Pro Tem

33

Bernice, Lousiana [Population 1,809]
Town Council, May 14 2002
Mildred Fergusin, Gene Terral, Minor Patton (Mayor), Joe Cusimano (Attorney), Lana Patton (Clerk), Elvin Dismuke & Rhodell Montgomery

Wadley, Georgia [Population 2,468]
City Council, August 13 2001
Izell Mack, Charles Lewis, Albert Samples (Mayor) & Robert Reeves (City Attorney)

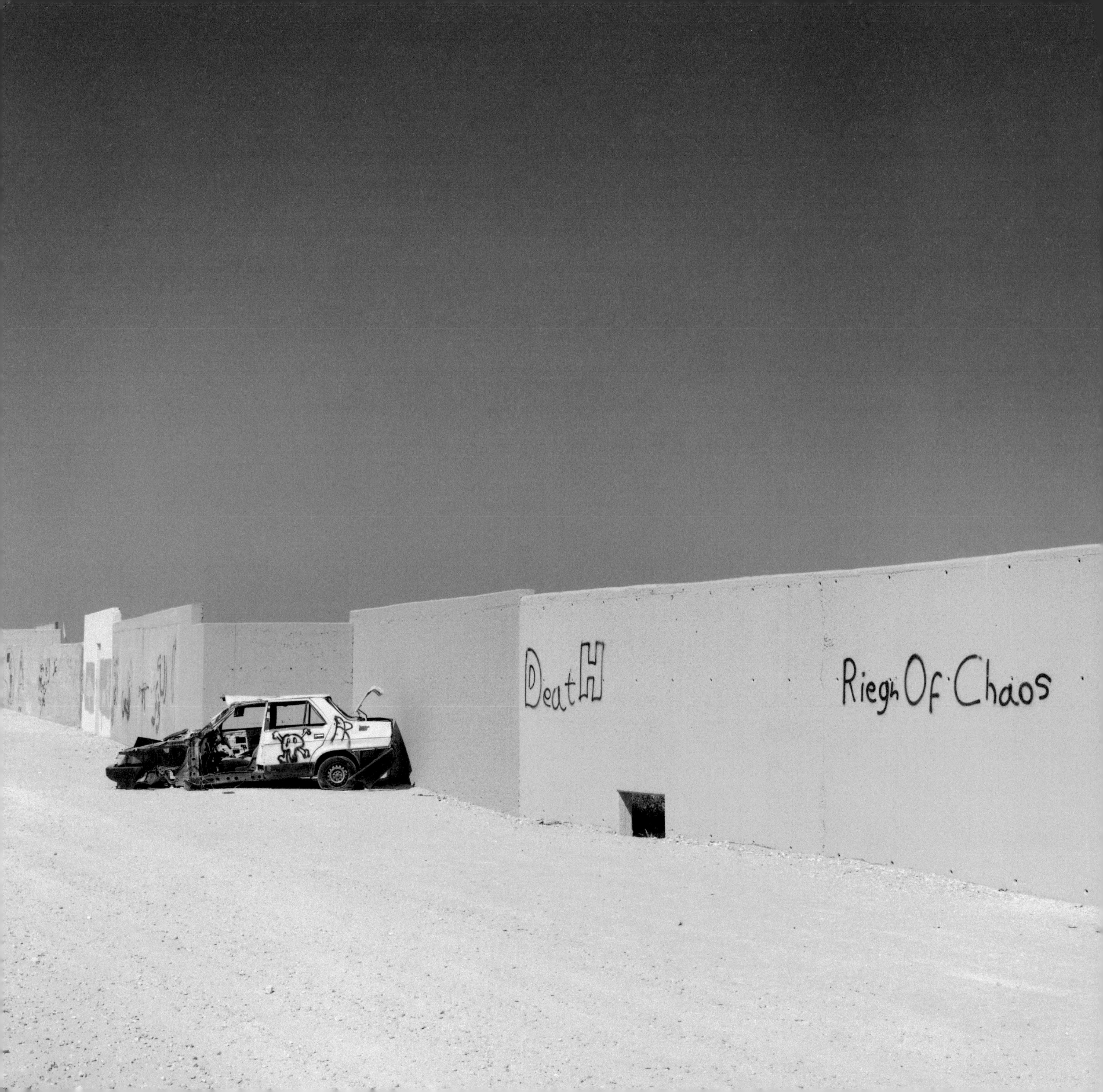
DeatH
Riegh Of Chaos

ADAM BROOMBERG AND OLIVER CHANARIN

Combining images from *Chicago*, a fake Arab town in the Negev desert built by the Israeli Defense Force for urban combat training, and *Bombs*, a series of reconstructions of suicide bombs disguised as innocuous everyday objects, Broomberg's and Chanarin's eclectic and narrative-led photographic work adds a new visual layer to the lexicon of politically charged social anthropology. Through this conflation of simulated places, buildings and objects, the overarching influence of military imperatives that continue to dominate and define almost all aspects of contemporary Israel begins to emerge.

Chicago 19

Bomb 4

Chicago

Chicago 28

Bomb 5

Bomb 3

(above) Chicago 2

(opposite) Bomb 1

(following pages) Bomb 2 and Chicago 4

CHIEN-CHI CHANG

The subject of alienation and connectivity between individuals is a recurring theme in the work of Chien-Chi Chang. These pictures from the series *Double Happiness* foreground the anxiety and uncertainty faced in brokered marriages between Taiwanese men and their Vietnamese brides. Through the nervous, unsmiling faces of the brides-to-be, standing or sitting awkwardly in anonymous waiting-rooms, Chang alerts us to the dehumanizing impact that a desire for economic security and future prosperity has on a growing number of deeply impoverished and disaffected Asian women.

SUSAN MEISELAS

Drawing inspiration from Meiselas's seminal book, *Nicaragua* (1981), *Re-Framing History* (2005) reworks some of the most potent and iconic images in a latter-day context. By physically and literally returning the images – re-fabricated on vinyl mesh material – to the original places where the pictures were made, the work speaks eloquently about the passage of time and its impact on communities living in sites of conflict and atrocity. *Re-Framing History* is, moreover, a multi-layered work, embracing conversations and impressions, provoked by the public installation, and recorded on video. This time-based project provides a salient link between those who experienced the trauma of revolution and those too young to remember it.

Managua, Nicaragua, July 2004

Mural: Somoza Portocarrero, 27-year-old son of the president and head of
the elite infantry training school (EEBI). Following a tradition of the United
States Army, the recruits celebrate graduation with *Schlitz* beer. April, 1979.

Estelí, Nicaragua, July 2004

Mural: National Guard entering Estelí. September, 1978.

(above) Monimbo, Nicaragua, July 2004

Mural: Youths throwing contact bombs in forest surrounding Monimbo. June, 1978.

(opposite) Matagalpa, Nicaragua, July 2004

Mural: Muchachos await counterattack by Somoza's National Guard. Matagalpa, 1978.

Masaya, Nicaragua, July 2004

Mural: Muchacho withdrawing from commercial district of
Masaya after three days of bombing. September, 1978.

MASAYA, 1979

Estelí, Nicaragua, July 2004

Mural: Fleeing the bombing to seek refuge outside of Estelí. September 20, 1978.

Managua, Nicaragua, July 2004
Mural: 'Cuesta del Plomo', hillside outside Managua, a well-known site
of many assassinations carried out by the National Guard. July, 1978.

WENG PEIJUN

Bird's Eye View and *Sitting On The Wall* are two bodies of work of simple pictorialism that utilize the same innocent motif to comment prophetically and powerfully on China's twenty-first century revolution: exponential urban growth. In the former, two schoolgirls on rooftops overlook the skylines of major cities; in the latter, a solitary girl sits uncomfortably on a wall and surveys the urban sprawl. With their backs to the camera, and literally facing their future, the girls represent the new generation of urban dwellers forced to contemplate the ominous redevelopment taking place in front of their eyes.

Bird's Eye View – Haikou

Bird's Eye View – Chongqing, 2004

Bird's Eye View – Guangzhou, 2004

Sitting on the Wall – Guangzhou 3

Sitting on the Wall – Guangzhou 4

Sitting on the Wall – Guangzhou 1

JULIO GRINBLATT

The idea of exclusion is central to the work of Julio Grinblatt, where the aura of not belonging, or of being a stranger, is a defining force in the artist's oeuvre. *People Facing Their Birthday Cakes* extends this sense of self-containment in an ironically engaging way. The graphic work deals with the stuff of magic, grounded in childhood memories. Contorted faces, illuminated only by candles, are transformed by the radiant light at the moment of a wish. Grinblatt's work is predicated on the decisive documentary moment, but he is less concerned with how the camera records reality and more with how the photochemical process gives substance and metaphorical significance to the ephemeral.

SHELBY LEE ADAMS

Appalachian Lives forms a new chapter in an ongoing body of work produced over a period of almost three decades, which reflects the photographer's deep and evolving engagement with the people of this region. Eschewing documentary objectivity, this unsentimental and brutally honest account of a marginalized community in the Appalachian Mountains – many of whom are friends and relatives of the photographer, who was born and grew up in the area – bears witness to a remote society at ease with itself and largely oblivious to the lure and technological trappings of the twenty-first century.

Tyler and Sheba, 2001

The Kitchen, 1997

Hylo's Place, 2000

Kelly Wayne, Faye and Shopper, 1997

The Nobles' Porch, 1999

Vertie Slone and Son, 2000

Driving Straight To Hell, 1998

SIMON NORFOLK

Hotel Africa was a folly, albeit an exorbitantly expensive one, created by the President of Liberia in 1979 to entertain the heads of state of the OAU. Now in ruins, following regime change, the empty blackened shell sits amongst a sea of refugee camps that surround the capital, Monrovia. Functioning today as the UN peacekeeping headquarters, the site has taken on a new mantle. In *Liberia: Welcome to the Hotel Africa*, Norfolk's rich and saturated pictures record the sanctity of the camp, a land of plenty, 24-hour electricity and military order, and its counterpart – on the other side of the fence – a country of total dereliction and impending anarchy.

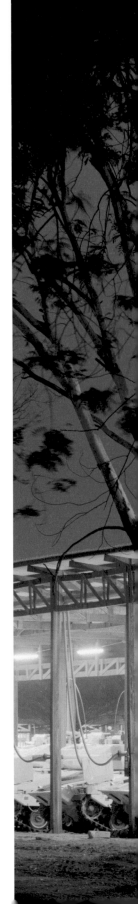

BORIS MIKHAILOV

Boris Mikhailov has for many years worked on the margins of ethical responsibility in relation to documentary reportage and the representation of the impoverished and dispossessed. Nonetheless, his abject subjects, who are very much representative of the social disintegration in Ukraine following the demise of the Soviet Union, offer an apposite metaphor for a country that escaped totalitarianism for the trappings of western-style democracy. Deeply harrowing and voyeuristic, these new portraits of the homeless, extend his controversial series and book, *Case History* (1997–8), and are not only a stark reminder of the plight of post-Soviet Ukraine, but are indicative of the social underbelly of all developed countries.

MICHAEL WESELY

For a significant part of his artistic career, Michael Wesely has been preoccupied with the structural properties of the photographic medium and, in particular, its capacity to accommodate unusually long exposure-times in one single image. Working with shutter speeds of anything up to four years, he began to apply his conceptual model to changes of urban structure and construction projects, such as the rebuilding of Potsdamer Platz in Berlin. In this context, his documentary approach directly parallels the time-based nature of the building process, where buildings that are demolished and constructed reverberate with uncertainty, paradoxically evoking erasure and regeneration simultaneously.

5.8.1999–6.12.2000 Leipziger Platz, Berlin

6.8.1999–6.12.2000 Leipziger Platz, Berlin

5.4.1997–3.6.1999 Potsdamer Platz, Berlin

27.3.1997—13.12.1998 Potsdamer Platz, Berlin

5.2.2003–28.4.2005 Kanadische Botschaft, Leipziger Platz, Berlin

TRENT PARKE

Street photography, once a bedrock of documentary practice, has been less visible in recent years, but there remain a number of practitioners who continually push at the boundaries of the genre: Trent Parke is one such photographer. Immersing himself in the rich urban setting of Sydney in Australia, Parke embarked on a photographic journey, lasting over five years, and produced *Dream/Life and Beyond* (1998–2002), an ethereal and mystical study of a city in a continual state of flux. Paradoxically heroic and furtive at the same time, Sydney's silent inhabitants, alternatively shrouded in acute darkness or glowing with iridescence, speak of a city in perpetual transition, spiritual growth and demographic change.

MASSIMO VITALI

Internationally recognized for his signature large-scale photographs of human interaction on Italian beaches and other public spaces, Massimo Vitali's luscious colour images apply a demographic clarity to the rites and rituals of modern leisure. The wealth of action that takes place on different levels within the picture plane, oblivious to the presence of the (physically distanced) artist, creates a framework of interpretation that belies the apparently simple narrative. Combining the wealth of detail afforded by view-camera photography with a fascination with the world of appearances, Vitali's work shifts seamlessly between the familiar realm of documentary realism and the surreal.

Calafuria

Rosignano, 2004

Rosignano Night

Mediumwave

Accademia

WHAT USE IS PHOTOGRAPHY?

MARTHA LANGFORD

Some thirty years ago, critic and novelist John Berger answered this question with a modest proposal. Addressing his comments to documentary photographers and characterizing photography as an instrument of record, he drew a parallel between photography and memory, urging respect for the laws of memory. Berger counselled documentary photographers to emulate amateur photographers whose pictures are seen and felt in a continuous present – whose pictures retain the contexts from which they were removed by the camera's cut. This occurs because private pictures are received by a community of collective memory. In a public photographic presentation – a meeting of strangers – the only viable replacement for collective memory's cohesion is a combination of words and images set in a radial structure that emulates the mental associations of recollection. In a word, context is key.[1]

Berger's system is anticipated and echoed in a multitude of theoretical constructs, some anything but modest. Communications theorist Marshall McLuhan's adaptation of Gestalt psychology's figure/ground formula shifts our attention from content to medium, and thereby argues the necessity to understand its shaping of consciousness.[2] With fewer certainties, perhaps, the *fin-de-siècle* and post-*fin-de-siècle* outpouring of photographic memory studies offers a myriad variations on Berger's contextual turn. More complications are added when reflexivity evolves from a position of critical distance to identification with Other, a feeling mistakable for love.[3] Words, expressed or withheld, symbolize the relational complexities of context – the ground truth, as it were. None of this is new, neither was originality claimed by Berger. Walter Benjamin had stated plainly the need for public photographs to be captioned, and explained the infinity of personal remembrance in relation to Proust.[4] A devout Benjaminian, Berger put his faith in the context of narrated time (storytelling), a poesis of factuality, that fused history and memory into a full showing and telling. Citing a poem by Bertolt Brecht, Berger promised the memory-minded documentary photographer that:

In this way
You will show the flow of events and also the course
Of your work, permitting the spectator
To experience this Now on many levels, coming from Previously and
Merging into Afterwards, also having much else Now
Alongside it.[5]

So Now Then, how have events flowed from Berger's time, now firmly in the Previously, into the Now of the common photographic era: post-structural, post-colonial, and post-photographic? Is there any Now left in the Afterwards? Was there any Then?

TRUTH IN TATTERS, REALITY IN RUINS

The movement and arrest that constitute the 'Now on many levels' – the intermingling of perception, imagination, and memory – previously meant that the photographic image could no longer be taken as transparent; or, rather, that transparency no longer stood in for truth. Now we are left with what really mattered to Berger, the complexity and elusiveness of truth. This needs to be said because showing and telling the truth still matters to many people who are not necessarily naive. Cultural theorists have long been spreading doubt about the legibility and reliability of photographic documents, an endless and thankless job that many were happy to quit when a new *post* was announced: the 'post-photographic era'.[6] In 1992, when William J. Mitchell's *Reconfigured Eye* was published, digital technology could be seen to have completed the work of post-structuralism: cutting the cord between image and external reality, blurring the distinction between fact and fiction, effectively casting the image in indeterminacy. The theoretical offshoots and visual harvests of these ideas have been bountiful; the uncanny and the improbable flourish, to disturb and entertain. Paradoxically, for this is hardly what Mitchell intended, an unquestioning acceptance of the post-photographic era results in a kind of epistemological and philosophical end-game: the photographic era can be treated as a discrete case-study of visual representation and reception (1839–1989 [7]) in the imaging industry's march of progress. Putting the tools of photographic manipulation and deception into everyone's hands should have brought debates over truth and falsehood to a close.

It will be obvious that this closure has nowhere occurred. Instead, we see signs of persistent faith in photographic evidence, however fragmented, pixelated, or otherwise mediated. The power of photography continues to be impressed on the general population by a variety of shocks, big and small: from the amateur photographs taken at Abu Ghraib prison to Princess Diana's 'death-by-photography'. In these well-known cases, the denotative truth-value of the pictures holds (the crumpled automobile struck by flash; the cringing bodies struck by flash), even as the context is ripped to shreds. By context, I mean precisely the kind of reference that I am making here which has come to disgust people who see the suffering of the victims (the princess, as well as the prisoners) eclipsed by propaganda and, most egregiously, by the musings of the cultural cadre. Furthermore, by starting with popular examples, I do not mean to imply that the intelligentsia have settled the issue of photographic truth; quite the contrary. Philosopher Avishai Margalit's definition of the 'moral witness' – courage and truthfulness embodied – might have to be expanded by Susan Sontag's about-face on the ethics of photojournalism; her prime example is a photo-fiction, her moral witnesses are mute, but her underlying point is that violence and atrocity are things that can be seen and photographed, and that this witnessing, while never fully understandable to non-witnesses, is the truth.[8] The irresolvable puzzle of novelist W.G. Sebald's photographic punctuation opens up another category of photographic truth. What we realize, as we become immersed in Sebald's universe, is that the pictures themselves, though plainly reproductions, are very important to us as photographic objects. We are interested in their provenance, but, more significantly, we are interested in their placement in the book. The images help us to negotiate a text about loss,

beginning with the loss of one's bearings. Indeed, the importance of these photographic objects as relics and signposts in the text is disproportionate to their denotative function; in comparison with the thickly descriptive text, the pictures, like Sontag's witnesses, are virtually mute. This realization throws us back to Roland Barthes's explanation of the reciprocal relationship between photographic imagery and text. Photographic connotation is 'quickened' by text, but the words 'are parasitic on the image', that is, the picture has to confirm the information conveyed by the words.[9] With Sebald, something quite different goes on, because neither the text nor the image is in the ascendant, nor is either intended to convey factual information. We are in the world of fiction, and we know it, so we are able to suspend disbelief and recognize the images as carriers of truth.[10] Our positions before these uses of photography suggest that *photogénie* has not been bred out by *photogenics*, or at least, that certain traits, or points of agreement, have not.[11]

First, the idea that truths are harboured in photographic tatters: this idea certainly holds strong as we continue to learn lessons from vernacular photography, especially the family album. We understand better the ambivalence and confusion that linger in private photographic documents, and how these conditions have been translated to photographic art. I am thinking of projects by Richard Billingham, Anna Fox and Nan Goldin, to name only a few. But these are only the most obvious examples of a tendency to mine categorical confusion by making the private public – a kind of bait-and-switch, in the sense that the spectator is drawn into the familiar and confronted by the Other. More relevant in the context of this book are long-term documentary projects that forge relationships between artists and communities for the duration. This sort of document-by-attachment has been produced since James Agee and Walker Evans headed south from New York City to live with tenant farmers. Though public (and very much intended for the public), social documentary projects, which are based on 'thin relations' (common humanity), effectively mimic the 'thick relations' of mnemonic communities – here again,

Notes

1 John Berger, 'Uses of Photography' (1978), in his *About Looking* (Pantheon Books, 1980), pp. 48–63.

2 Marshall McLuhan, *Understanding Media: The Extensions of Man* (McGraw-Hill, 1964). The context of McLuhan, including 'New Criticism and British Cultural Studies', is explained by Janine Marchessault in *Marshall McLuhan: Cosmic Media* (Sage Publications, 2005), pp. 2–34.

3 See Marianne Hirsch, 'Projected Memory: Holocaust Photographs in Personal and Public Fantasy', in Mieke Bal, Jonathan Crewe and Leo Spitzer (eds), *Acts of Memory: Cultural Recall in the Present* (Dartmouth College, 1999), pp. 2–23. Hirsch refers to Kaja Silvermann's concept of 'identification-at-a-distance', developed in her *Threshold of the Visible World* (Routledge, 1996).

4 Walter Benjamin, 'Little History of Photography' (1931) and 'On the Image of Proust' (1929), in his *Selected Writings*, vol. 2, ed. Michael W. Jennings (Belknap Press of Harvard University Press, 1999), pp. 527, 238.

5 Berger, 'Uses of Photography', p. 61.

6 William J. Mitchell, *The Reconfigured Eye: Visual Truth in the Post-Photographic Era* (MIT Press, 1994).

7 Mitchell gives the life-span of photography as 150 years. 'From the moment of its sesquicentennial in 1989, photography was dead – or, more precisely, radically and permanently displaced – as was painting 150 years before.' See ibid., p. 20.

8 Avishai Margalit's concept of the 'moral witness' excludes most war correspondents, though Margalit admits those whose testimony has a moral purpose. See *The Ethics of Memory* (MIT Press, 2002), p. 151. Susan Sontag's softening of her position on photojournalists, especially war photographers, appears in *Regarding the Pain of Others* (Farrar, Straus and Giroux, 2003).

9 Roland Barthes, 'The Photographic Message' (1961), from *Image-Music-Text*, trans. Stephen Heath (1978), in Susan Sontag (ed.), *A Barthes Reader* (Hill and Wang, 1983), pp. 204–5.

10 W.G. Sebald's incorporation of photographs into both fiction and non-fiction is well known. Every reader of Sebald has a favourite: mine is *The Emigrants*, trans. Michael Hulse (New Directions, 1997).

I am indebted to Margalit.[12] The curious thing is that 'thick relations' are now found to be latent in these products of 'thin relations', as my final remarks will show.

A second surviving aspect of photography is the sense that photographic realities are constituted in small deaths. 'The image', says Eduardo Cadava, is 'composed of ruin, belonging to ruin, taking its point of departure from ruin, seeking to speak of ruin, and not only its own – "but also the ruin of ruin" '.[13] Some see the medium itself as a tattered ruin. Rosalind E. Krauss heartily asserts that 'now photography can only be viewed through the undeniable fact of its own obsolescence'.[14] This fact constitutes the frame, or context, of all contemporary photographic experience. Our knowledge of digital photographic technology – the very real possibility that a photograph has been tampered with, completely or partially constructed – turns the photographic prospect into a lost horizon. We no longer feel in possession of the facts, and, as I've argued elsewhere, 'we have adjusted our thinking to a photography that warns us of our dispossession'.[15] Are further adjustments possible and desirable? I think they are, in ways that restore the usefulness of the medium. Considering the photographic image as something *like* reality – replacing the posture of witnessing with the blatant imposture that poses the question 'what if?' – places all photography under the rule of fiction, that is, in a context of the imaginable. Representation thus becomes the representation of a possible reality, a visual thought completed by the imagination, and something to talk about. What if these images of atrocity were true? What moral position should I take? To adopt this attitude is to realize that photography has always been used in this way, whether to prompt stories or catalyse debate, though not necessarily by all. Throughout this essay, I have generally been referring to one group of subjects: Berger's spectators and their descendants. The other subjects one might consider are the people pictured in the photographic objects. *Pace* McLuhan, let me be very literal, for just a moment. Let me shift your attention from ground to figure.

TOUCHING AND NAMING

First, the object: the materiality of the photographic object, including its scale and tactility, is of increasing interest to photographic theorists and historians. Fascinated as we still are with the photograph, we are venturing outside the boundaries of vision to consider photographic experience as a richer mode of consciousness, informed and affected by the entire sensorium. Geoffrey Batchen has studied the importance of touch to western photographic experience, looking at pictures of people holding and looking at pictures, as well as at the tactility of photographic jewellery, reliquaries and albums. His study is concerned with remembrance, and tinged with loss.[16] Chris Wright's compelling essay on the life of photographic relics in the Western Solomon Islands reports more activity in the present. In the case of a bereaved son, 'the photograph is a powerful relic that retains a physical, bodily connection to his father; it partakes of his father's substance'.[17] Linking these two studies is the quality of uniqueness. The photographs that Batchen finds incorporated into three-dimensional objects, or given symbolic framing, become unique objects. They are auratic. In Roviana, Wright discovers that the reproducibility of the photograph is essentially unknown. There are almost no negatives, to this day – the Roviana people treat photographs of their ancestors as precious objects, carrying forward beliefs about embodiment that predated the introduction of Christian memorial practices. The photographic likeness keeps the bereaved in contact with the departed; they can continue to talk.[18] While Wright's findings are particular to Roviana, he invites us to consider whether European and North American conversion to digital media might not imbue the photographic print with the same auratic presence. Perhaps, but what we are hearing now is quite the opposite: that powerful encounters are taking place through digital technology.

Nunavut is a Canadian territory that comprises one-fifth of the nation's landmass, running north and west of Hudson's Bay, above the tree-line, to the North Pole.

11 *Photogénie, photogenia*, or the genius of photography, is a term used by sociologist Edgar Morin for the cumulative effect of photography, qualities that are in fact 'properties of our mind … The richness of the photograph is in fact all that is not there, but that we project or fix onto it.' See Morin's *Cinema, or The Imaginary Man*, trans. Lorraine Mortimer (University of Minnesota Press, 2005), p. 22. 'Photogenics' is the title of an essay on electronic reproduction by Geoffrey Batchen, *History of Photography*, 22/1 (1998), reprinted in Liz Wells (ed.), *The Photography Reader* (Routledge, 2004), pp. 228–39.

12 For his distinction between thick (communal; ethical) and thin (human; moral) relations, and their connections with memory, see Margalit, *The Ethics of Memory*, pp. 7, 18–47.

13 Eduardo Cadava, 'Lapsus Imaginis: The Image in Ruins', *October*, 96 (Spring 2001), 35.

14 Rosalind E. Krauss, 'Reinventing the Medium', *Critical Inquiry*, 25 (Winter 1999), 289.

15 Martha Langford, 'Lost Horizons, or the Gates Close at Sunset: Doubtful Realisms and Paradisiacal Gains', in Martha Langford (ed.), *Image & Imagination* (McGill-Queen's University Press, 2005), pp. 114–27. My exploration of the 'like' draws on Paul Ricoeur, 'The Metaphorical Process as Cognition, Imagination, and Feeling', *Critical Inquiry*, 5 (Autumn 1978), 142–59.

16 Geoffrey Batchen, *Forget Me Not: Photography and Remembrance* (Van Gogh Museum and Princeton Architectural Press, 2004).

17 Chris Wright, 'Material and Memory: Photography in the Western Solomon Islands', *Journal of Material Culture*, 9(1), 76.

18 Ibid., 82.

19 *http://www.collectionscanada.ca/inuit/054301-e.html*. Site visited on 9 April 2006.

20 Berger, 'Uses of Photography', pp. 56–7.

21 The portrait identified through *Project Naming* is not the same frame as was used in *The Family of Man*. The image identified can be accessed through the *Project Naming* website. See note 17.

Created in 1999, Nunavut is the Inuit homeland. Photographs of the Canadian Arctic and its people have been produced since the 1870s, recording expeditions, commercial exploitation and missionary activities. Both professionals and amateurs have contributed to this photographic heritage, which is largely held in the south. Portraiture represents a substantial portion of these collections, though, as we might expect from the colonizer's archives, the names of the depicted are missing. In 2001, *Project Naming* was initiated, an archives project completely dependent on digital technology.[19] Photographs of Inuit people taken by Richard Harrington at Kugluktuk (formerly Coppermine), Padlei, Taloyoak (formerly Spence Bay), and Igloolik (Iglulik) during the late 1940s and early 1950s were scanned. Then, college students from Nunavut Sivuniksavut, equipped with CD-ROMs and laptops, visited the Elders of these communities to ask for their help in identifying the figures. From these digital images, the names came, and with the names came stories.

As many times as I have read Berger's essay, I always stumble over his equivocal analysis of *The Family of Man*. Crediting curator Edward Steichen's intuition that 'private uses of photography can be exemplary for their public use', and conceding that this experiment had failed, Berger nevertheless clings to his hope that the 'distinction between the private and the public uses of photography would be transcended. *The Family of Man* would exist.'[20] Few Canadian photographers took part in *The Family of Man*. Harrington's photographs of the Arctic were selected, including a photograph of a Padlemiut woman in labour. In the book, the image is identified simply as 'Arctic'.

Then, the scenes were presented as timeless and universal. Now, this photograph could be entitled *Utnguuyaq in labour* (1950), and accompanied by the information that 'In the past, women assisted with the delivery of babies.'[21] So, have Berger's hopes been realized? On many levels, they have. A figure from the past re-encountered on a computer screen is the occasion for intergenerational transmission. More than simply naming, the project forms a bond between Elder and interviewer: the young participants say this. A photographic album never loses its charm.

But the fusion of public and private photography has never taken place, and never will. The private photograph that migrates into the public assumes a public function, as a site for speculation about the state of the world. What if? The public photograph that returns to the private realm becomes a meeting point for a mnemonic community. *This is how it was*. These uses of photography mirror each other; they mimic each other as alternative ways of thinking about the world. We should cling to these nuances through thick and thin.

LOOK AND TELL: SOME FURTHER THOUGHTS ON THE DOCUMENTARY GENRE

JAN-ERIK LUNDSTRÖM

Why documentary practices? Can we produce a reasonable working definition, or is there even a somewhat cohesive family of practices that may be brought together under the umbrella of this one concept? What do we make of the calls for a 'return to the real', or, at the core of contemporary popular culture, of the insatiable demand for staged and fictive 'reality' (in order not to be confronted with the real itself)?

At a seminar recently a delegate claimed to have reached a state of documentary fatigue (this is not a position you may take outside the art world), pointing to the 'over-bearing presence of documentary works at the latest Documenta' and all the fuss appearing about the documentary mode in more or less chic art magazines of the day. Yes, there might be a documentary boom (just as there is a backlash, more or less simultaneously; 'the stigma of politics has never been greater than now', as Martha Rosler says in a recent interview[1]). And the boom looks different, as most things do, depending upon your viewpoint, your worldview, your values. So let's put it this way: it is hard to think politics, hard to think the present, think social space, think public action, think response and resistance, think opposition and concurrence, think knowledge, think doubt, think solidarity and think love, think certainty and think potentiality, without thinking documentary work, without thinking the document.

From journalism to popular culture to fine arts to the human and empirical sciences, the document holds territory, even though from time to time scoffed at or re-embraced by the market, run over by neo-liberal ideologues who rework Marx's notion of 'all that is solid melts into the air' to laissez-faire positions in relation to any political change, cut short in the harsh battle over ruling paradigms in the feverishly globalizing present. There is little reason to doubt the continued presence and power and impact of documentary practices, unless we doubt the survival of public discourse and public space altogether. Which we might.

But, again, is there any longer an identifiable documentary genre, given the current proliferation of methodologies, approaches, positions, practices? The documentary genre was named (and its naming, identifying it as an expansive and particular mode of operation, responded to a historical context where notions of reportage and journalism developed as photographic media expanded their repertoire) and evolved during the course of the twentieth century. From time to time, the genre's uneasy or contested relationship to and/or within the visual arts is best described as ideological. Read Elizabeth McCausland in *Photo Notes*, the year is 1939, claiming documentary photography as the new photography, having even made irrelevant the question of whether photography is art:

> Against this pattern of sterility, of ideas which could not reproduce themselves, we have the new function (and evolving from it, the new aesthetic) of documentary photography, an application of photography direct and realistic, dedicated to the profound and sober chronicling of the external world.

And,

> For the greatest objective of such work is to widen the world we live in, to acquaint us with the range and variety of human existence, to inform us (as it were forcibly) of unnecessary social horrors such as war, to make us aware of the civilization in which we live and hope to function as creative workers. This is useful work, and as such beyond claims of mere personality or clique.[2]

McCausland's celebration of documentary photography, inscribing it in opposition to pictorialism, Romanticism and even early modernism in general, an opposition many will still subscribe to, however shadows another, often misunderstood or ignored, historical narrative. As, for example, Bill Nichols has shown, in his theoretical/historical work on documentary film, the documentary genre was dependent upon aesthetic developments within early modernism (Eisensteinian montage, Brechtian *Verfremdung*, Rodchenko's

fig. 8   fig. 9

upsetting of perspective, Man Ray's impurification of the photographic medium, etc.).[3] Rather than opposition, the relationship turns out to be one of influence, affiliation and rapport. The documentary genre was born in synchronicity with modernism; its twin, if we so wish, purchasing and chasing time and space and human life, both in competition with and on behalf of modernism's grandest narratives.

The link to contemporary practices of a self-reflexive and self-conscious work is clear, meta-documentary works making precise commentary on the genre, is not far-fetched. Leif Claesson literally probes what it is like to be in someone else's clothes (fig. 8 & 9) as in the work *c/o* he asks the fundamental and thorny documentary questions: Who is speaking thus for whom? Can I/may I/should I speak for you? Who am I who is doing the speaking? Dressing himself in the clothes of the homeless, evacuating them from the picture (the homeless are represented through their absence), Claesson oversteps the safe physical boundaries of representation and documentation. In involving his own body he makes the viewer painfully and uncomfortably aware of the real powers and stakes of documentary work; there is no outside to representation.

Similarly, both in still photographs and in a video piece, *Turn On* by Adrian Paci tunes in to meta-documentary questions. Again, the paradigmatic subject of the documentary tradition – the homeless, the outcast, the marginalized, the social Other – is sighted and observed and photographed: in this case unemployed men from Shkodra, Paci's Albanian home-town. Given the unreliable supply of electricity, a group of men from the streets are given an electric generator with which they are able to light up a light bulb. Which is exactly what they do. Noisy rambling old electrical generators work to produce light. And these unemployed men supply the action, symbolically and metaphorically not only generating light, but generating and controlling their own image, contrary to much of documentary tradition. *Turn On* empowers on two levels, first in the real world, then in the image.

The assertion of modernism's place in the evolution of the documentary genre points out another, perhaps even more fundamental fact: the path towards factual descriptions of reality passes through the processes of aesthetic fiction. Documentary truths are and have always been and will always be constructions. There is no outside to aesthetic processing where documentary could propose itself to stand. Yes, this is nothing new (but we tend to forget this fact as we argue for the authenticity of documentary, as opposed to the inauthenticity of art). Already Theodor Adorno knew this. Social facts were, for him, best addressed obliquely; no one, in his eyes, conceived of capitalist societies' inherent maladies more clearly than Franz Kafka, whose fables unmasked both the political and the social system – including the infrastructure of the economy – without ever naming it. Thus, for Adorno, redemption and reconciliation is not the purpose of art. Rather, art is inextricably tied to the irreconciled world we all inhabit. 'The notion of the perfect work cancels the concept of art itself…' for 'the quality of an art work is largely determined by whether or not it meets the challenge of the irreconcilable.'[4]

Irredeeming and masterfully discordant, Owen Logan, in the forty-three-photograph-long sequence *Masquerade: Nigeria Hits Michael Jackson*, tells the fan-tastic story of finding Michael Jackson's twin brother in Nigeria. Multi-layered ironies, insider and outsider commentary, choreographed in poignant black-and-white tableaux, drive a sophisticated and complex political narrative on the post-colonial oil-coloured landscape of the Nigerian present. Borders between fact and fiction, straight photography and manipulation, documentary and theatre, empathy and attack are perfectly seamless; conceptual drive meets with exuberant storytelling.

Extending friction and resistance, the Atlas Group manages a fictional or pseudo-fictional – and real – archive 'documenting' the Lebanese civil war, 1975–90, in effect a war between Israel/USA and Syria. A key target of this war was the Lebanese capital Beirut. And it is Beirut that is the focus of the Atlas Group's archive. The particular repertoire

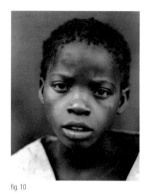

fig. 10   fig. 11

(fig. 8 & 9) Care Of diptych © Leif Claesson

(fig. 10) Rebecca Mulinga © Lukas Einsele

(fig. 11) Angola Group Portrait © Lukas Einsele

of violence of this war is chartered and displayed by the Atlas Group Archive – the car bomb, the hostage, the sniper from above; all of these are detailed, examined, recreated, realized. Exceptionally precise 'documents' appear in the archive, chronicling, for example, each and every car bomb in Beirut throughout this period, including information about the kind of car and the amount of explosives used.[5] No real archive could tell more about the reality of the war than this fictional archive. Or? The layers of real and fictive are a hall of mirrors… We could also claim that since the facts only exist through the work of the archive, we, as viewers, visitors, co-producers, complicits, can, must, in the end, get involved with documenting, assessing, comprehending this particular war ourselves.

Did we then answer that stubborn question 'what is documentary?' Often, the genre's mode of being has been linked to the supposed transparency of the photographic sign, its indexicality, in Peirce's terminology. Grounded in the false opposition between 'art' and 'documentary', familiar dualist distinctions have been put to use: mirror and trace, opacity and transparency, window and landscape in Barthes's poetic differentiation; documentary always casting its vote on the indexical team. Yet, given the above interdependence between early experimental modernism, forwarding practices of opacity or construction, and the rise of the documentary genre, we may leave indexicality aside, suffice with it being a possible but not necessary condition. And, given that a singular epistemology or ontology of the photograph is no longer possible, a technical definition of documentary is not workable. My inclination is to steer towards a non-technical definition, to suggest that the core of the documentary genre we find not in the medium's properties or in the conditions established by a particular technology, or in this or that style or even working method, it is not about manipulation or not, or of bearing witness or not. It is, rather, about identifying a particular attention to the world, a will to know and a desire to immerse, an attentiveness and alertness; a training upon, a leaning towards, a forward movement. Certainly, the verbs related to vision – look, observe, gaze, scrutinize,

view, sight, spot, eye, recognize and regard – bring us along a path of possibilities; especially if we understand this attentiveness as generative, interventive, productive, transformative. And just as productivity includes the possibility of failure, sight also contains the possibility of non-sight, of blindness, of the failure to see.

The documentary genre remains a key site for a number of central concerns of human culture. Not only does it embody a complex dialectic between fact and subject position, record and interpretation, observation and analysis; it is also the platform for issues such as the epistemology of the image, the production and dissemination of knowledge, questions of agency, truth, objectivity and subjectivity, the ethics of representation and of looking, identity politics, issues of experience versus analysis, fact and fiction, the observer's relationship to the observed, discursive hierarchies and processes of victimization and stigmatization, questions of who is speaking what and for whom. Precisely when confronting documentary practices, we are thrown straight into such crucial issues of the image.

Given this range of issues, it is clearly not possible to gather contemporary documentary practices under one single rubric. Contemporary documentaries are affirmative and disillusioned, pragmatic and utopian, are often impure, hybrid, layered, combinatory, contradictory or unresolved. They treat facts, articulate information, interpret the record; they stage the real and observe the staged; meet factuality with fantasy, detailed observations with imagination. Scientific (or pseudo-scientific) scrutiny of subject matter blends with theatrical baroque narrative. Overall, a growing, expansive and rich toolbox is available for the documentary artist; choose or create what suits your project. Even topicality is allowed.

Who would think, for example, that a documentary project, enlisting still photographs and texts, would be *the* work of and about globalization? Allan Sekula's *Fish Story*, consisting in its entirety of seven chapters of sequences of still photographs/texts

Notes

1   Martha Rosler, 'Bringing it all back home', *Frieze*, November–December 2005, 92–9.

2   Elizabeth McCausland, 'Documentary photography', *Photo Notes*, January, 1939.

3   Bill Nichols, *Representing Reality: Issues and Concepts in Documentary* (Indiana University Press, 1991); Bill Nichols, *Introduction to Documentary* (Indiana University Press, 2001).

4   Theodor Adorno, *Aesthetic Theory* (Routledge, 1984), p. 271.

5   *www.theatlasgroup.org.*

6   Allan Sekula, *Fish Story* (Richter Verlag, 1996). This work of Sekula is of course preceded by works such as *Canadian Notes*, and followed by *Dismal Science*.

7   Karen Knorr, *Marks of Distinction* (Thames & Hudson, 1991). See also *www.karenknorr.com.*

8   Paul Ricoeur, *Oneself as Another* (University of Chicago Press, 1992); Dominick LaCapra, *Writing History, Writing Trauma* (Johns Hopkins University Press, 2001).

9   *www.one-step-beyond.de.*

10 Susan Meiselas, *Nicaragua* (Pantheon, 1980); *Kurdistan: In the Shadow of History* (Random House, 1997); *Encounters with the Dani* (Steidl, 2003); *www.akakurdistan.com, www.susanmeiselas.com.*

This text develops some of the themes in the author's essay *After the Fact*, in the publication of the same name, published by the Berlin Photography Festival, Berlin, 2005.

and two slide sequences, discovers and investigates, through the prism of the sea, the processes and the consequences of globalization.[6] No exclusively textual account has told more about globalization than this work, which travels the continents and manages both to bring the sea back into modernity and to manifest and work through the globalizing economy, through photographs equally seductive and analytic.

Likewise, a contemporary classic, Karen Knorr's series of photographic sequences – *Belgravia, Gentlemen, Country Life, Connoisseurs* and *Capital* – remain milestones when it comes to the comprehension of the powers of photography in narrating and displaying culture, and to the reinvention of documentary practices in photography. Re-aiming the camera horizontally and upwardly, Knorr both reworks relations of image and text and collapses notions of inside and outside.[7]

From a parallel perspective, a cluster of concepts focusing on human inter-relations are at the core of documentary discourse: the possibilities and traps of empathy, of identification and affiliation, speaking for or against, of engagement, alliance and solidarity. Paul Ricoeur's impelling call for a path for the affective imagination, to enounce and animate the social while we 'project ourselves into the lives of others' and Dominick LaCapra's challenging notion of 'empathetic unsettlement' capture something essential about contemporary modes of engagement.[8] Look at Lukas Einsele's *A Step Beyond/The Mine Revisited* (fig. 10 & 11) which is a complexly layered confrontation with landmines and their victims, orchestrated through visiting the four most mined countries of the world – Afghanistan, Angola, Bosnia and Cambodia.[9] Attending the aftermath and the consequences, Einsele reads history backwards, like Benjamin, and reinvites the empathetic imagination, as photographs and other records represent these particular landscapes of terror and, moreover, the fate of individuals as regards mines. Remarkable is the broad repertoire – the application of written and spoken text, filmed interviews, portraits of the mines themselves, drawings done by the mine victims, etc. Conceptually eloquent, each individual story is narrated with identical ingredients, forwarding both similarities and differences. The past of the mine accident is empowered through skilful use of the temporal grammar of the still photograph itself; it is a work of the history of the present.

Susan Meiselas's *Re-Framing History* also revisits contested historical sites, in her case the Sandinista revolution in Nicaragua. Here the historical documentation includes Meiselas's very own photographs, gathered in the book/exhibition *Nicaragua* from 1981. Physically returning her own photographs, installing them as murals publicly on the sites where they were photographed, *Re-Framing History* explores the passage of time since the revolution and people's memories, dreams lost and found, hopes as regards their country. Simultaneously a particular history of human and political engagement is re-presented, adding layers and perspective to our present.

Significant in Meiselas's photographic oeuvre is her replete exploration of the way photographs partake in telling, narrating and creating civil society. If her own photographs have followed and examined tumultuous events in late twentieth century societies, her project *Kurdistan: In the Shadow of History* tells the previously untold history of the Kurdish people through the meticulous gathering of professional and amateur photographs from all possible sources. Commitment, resourcefulness, patience and visual intelligence make this unprecedented kind of photographic history possible. Website joins with major monograph in meeting the parameters of this project. *Encounters with the Dani*, likewise inventive, makes use of the entire photographic record of anthropological and, later, traveller, tourist, colonizer and commercial encounters with the Dani people from New Guinea, masterfully investigating the complex consequences both of those encounters in and of themselves and of their representation.[10] The panorama of ways of attending the world and the bountiful register of empathetic presence take us back to the momentum of this publication: the rich complexity of contemporary documentary practices.

BIOGRAPHIES

SHELBY LEE ADAMS, born Hazard, Kentucky, USA, 1950; currently lives and works in Massachusetts, USA. He gained an MA in Photography at University of Iowa (1975) and a MFA in Photography at Massachusetts College of Art, Boston (1989). His work is represented in numerous permanent collections all over the world and has been widely exhibited, including recent solo shows in New York and New Orleans, USA, Toronto, Canada and Lausanne, Switzerland. He has had several monographs published about his work and has received awards such as the Photography Fellowship from the National Endowment for the Arts, Washington DC, and the Peter S. Reed Photography Grant.
Nominated for *So Now Then* by Alissa Schoenfeld, Yossi Milo Gallery, New York.

ADAM BROOMBERG AND OLIVER CHANARIN, born South Africa, 1970, and UK, 1971; the artists are currently based in London. Together they have produced four photographic books: *Trust* (2000), which accompanied their solo show at the Hasselblad Center; *Ghetto* (2003); and *Mr Mkhize's Portrait* (2004), which accompanied their solo show at the Photographers' Gallery, London. Their next book, *Chicago*, will be published by Steidl in autumn 2006. Commissions include the National Portrait Gallery, the Soros Foundation, the Arts Council of England and Photoworks, UK. They continue to work for a number of magazines, including the *Guardian Weekend*, the *Observer Magazine* and *Life*. Last year they produced their first film, commissioned by Channel 4.
Nominated for *So Now Then* by Anne Braybon, National Portrait Gallery, London.

CHIEN-CHI CHANG, born Taiwan, 1961; gained a BA from Soochow University, Taiwan (1984) and his MSc at Indiana University, USA (1990) before becoming a staff photographer for the *Seattle Times* and later the *Baltimore Sun*. He currently lives and works in Taipei and New York and is a member of Magnum Photos. He has exhibited widely, including Columbus Museum of Art, Ohio; the International Center of Photography, New York; the São Paulo Biennale; and the Venice Biennale. His publications include *I do I do I do* (2001), *The Chain* (2002) and *Double Happiness* (2005). He is a recipient of the W. Eugene Smith Memorial Fund for Humanistic Photography.
Nominated for *So Now Then* by Lesley Martin, *Aperture* magazine, USA.

JULIO GRINBLATT, born Buenos Aires, Argentina, 1960; currently lives and works in New York. He gained a BSc in Chemistry and Biochemistry in the Hebrew University of Jerusalem (1984). His work has been widely exhibited, including: Ruth Benzacar Gallery, Buenos Aires; Baró Cruz Gallery, São Paulo; Laura Marsiaj Contemporary Art, Rio de Janeiro; Slought Foundation, Philadelphia; Society for Contemporary Photography, Kansas City; and Museum of Modern Art, Buenos Aires. His work is featured in publications including: *People Facing Their Birthday Cakes*, Blue Sky Gallery, Portland; *Más allá del documento*, Museo Reina Sofía, Madrid; *Mapas abiertos*, Lunwerg, Barcelona; and *Blink*, Phaidon, UK.
Nominated for *So Now Then* by Chris Boot, Chris Boot Publishing, London, UK.

AN-MY LÊ, born Saigon, Vietnam, 1960; she came to the United States in 1975 as a refugee. She gained an MFA from Yale University School of Art in 1993. Recent solo exhibitions of her work include: *29 Palms* at Murray Guy Gallery, New York; and *Small Wars* at PS1/MOMA Contemporary Art Center, New York. She is the recipient of a John Simon Guggenheim Memorial Foundation Fellowship (1997), and her work is represented in a number of major collections including: the Museum of Modern Art, New York; San Francisco Museum of Modern Art; Metropolitan Museum of Art, New York; and Bibliothèque Nationale, Paris.
Nominated for *So Now Then* by Richard Woodward, photography critic, New York, USA.

SUSAN MEISELAS, born USA, 1948; gained a BA from Sarah Lawrence College and an MA in Visual Education from Harvard University. She currently lives and works in New York. She has had numerous solo exhibitions, in Madrid, Amsterdam, London, Los Angeles, Chicago and New York. A leading member of Magnum Photos, her work is represented in many American and international collections. Honorary awards of recognition include: the Robert Capa Gold Medal, Overseas Press Club (1979); the Leica Award for Excellence (1982); the Engelhard Award from the Institute of Contemporary Art (1985); the Maria Moors Cabot Prize from Columbia University (1994); and the Hasselblad Foundation International Photography Award (1994). She was made a MacArthur Fellow in 1992.
Nominated for *So Now Then* by Russell Roberts, Curator, National Museum of Photography, Film and Television, Bradford, UK.

BORIS MIKHAILOV, born Kharkov, Ukraine, 1938; currently lives and works in Kharkov and Berlin. His work has been widely exhibited, including shows at: the Saatchi Gallery and Tate Modern, London; Photographic Museum, Helsinki; Centre de la Photographie, Geneva; Institute of Contemporary Art, Boston; Institute Culturade Barcelona, Spain; Palau de la Virreina, Barcelona; Museu Serralves, Porto; Stedelijk Museum, Amsterdam; and MOMA, New York. His work has been published in numerous monographs and books. He won the Hasselblad Foundation International Photography Award (2000) and the Citibank Photography Prize, London (2001).
Nominated for *So Now Then* by Chris Killip, Harvard University, USA.

SIMON NORFOLK, born Lagos, Nigeria, 1963. He gained BA degrees from Oxford and Bristol Universities in Social Anthropology and Philosophy and Sociology, and went on to study Documentary Photography at Gwent College, Newport (1988). He currently lives and works in London. His work has been shown internationally, including solo exhibitions at: Bonni Benrubi Gallery, New York; Photographers' Gallery, London; Les Rencontres d'Arles; FotoFest, Houston; and Gallery Luisotti, Santa Monica. His work is held in numerous permanent collections, and he has been the recipient of major awards and prizes, including the Infinity Award, International Center for Photography, New York, and the European Publishers' Award for Photography.
Nominated for *So Now Then* by Dewi Lewis, Dewi Lewis Publishing, UK.

TRENT PARKE, born Newcastle, New South Wales, Australia, 1971. He currently lives in Sydney. His work has been exhibited widely, including recent solo exhibitions in Sydney, New York and Germany. He won the prestigious W. Eugene Smith Award for Humanistic Photography (2003) and a World Press Photo Award (1999, 2000, 2001 and 2005). He was also selected to be part of the World Press Photo Masterclass (1999). He self-published his first two books *Dream/Life* (1999) and, with Narelle Autio, *The Seventh Wave* (2000). He is an associate member of Magnum Photos, and is represented by Stills Gallery, Sydney.
Nominated for *So Now Then* by Alasdair Foster, Director, Australian Centre of Photography, Sydney.

WENG PEIJUN (also known as Weng Fen), born Hainan, China, 1961; graduated from Guangzhou Academy of Fine Arts, Guangzhou, China in 1985. He currently lives and works in Hainan/Beijing. His work has been frequently exhibited internationally, including: International Center of Photography, New York; Pompidou Centre, Paris; Kaohsiung Museum of Fine Art, Kaohsiung, Taiwan; Mori Art Museum, Toyko; Tamaya Museum, Mexico; Shanghai Art Museum, Shanghai; Guangdong Mueum of Art, Guangzhou; and Marella Contemporary Art, Milan, Italy. His work is represented in many permanent collections, including: International Center of Photography, New York; Hanart TZ Gallery,

Hong Kong; Pompidou Centre, Paris; Arhus Kunstmuseum, Arhus, Denmark; and Shanghai Museum, China.
Nominated for *So Now Then* by Paul Wombell, independent curator and Director of Hereford Photography Festival, UK, 2006.

PAUL SHAMBROOM, born Teaneck, New Jersey, USA, 1956; he lives and works in Minneapolis, Minnesota. Solo exhibitions include: Julie Saul Gallery, New York; Museum of Contemporary Photography, Chicago; Nederlands Fotomuseum, Rotterdam; Arles Rencontres de la Photographie; Rocket Gallery, London Fotographie Forum International, Frankfurt and Walker Art Center, Minneapolis. He has received grants and fellowships from, among others: the Guggenheim Foundation; Penny McCall Foundation and the Creative Capital Foundation. Shambroom's work is included in many collections including: Whitney Museum and the Museum of Modern Art, New York; Art Institute of Chicago; San Francisco Museum of Modern Art; and the Museum of Fine Arts, Boston. Publications include, *Face to Face with the Bomb: Nuclear Reality After the Cold War* (2003) and *Meetings* (2004).
Nominated for *So Now Then* by Chuck Samuels, Administrative Director, Le Mois de la Photo, Montreal, Canada.

MASSIMO VITALI, born Como, Italy, 1944. Studied at London College of Printing, UK, in 1964. He currently lives and works in Lucca, Italy. He has had solo shows in numerous places worldwide, including Bonni Benrubi Gallery, New York; Arndt & Partner, Berlin; Hilger Contemporary, Vienna; Lentos Kunstmuseum, Linz; Museo-C-Arte Luigi Pecci, Prato. His work is held in many permanent collections, including: Guggenheim Collection, New York; Museum of Contemporary Art, Denver; Fond National Art Contemporaine, Paris; Centre Pompidou – Musée National d'Art Moderne Paris; Arken Museum, Denmark; Ella Fontanals Cisneros Collection, USA; Museo de Arte contemporaneo de Castilla y Leon; Fondazione Sandretto Rebaudengo, Guarene, Turin; Sammlung E-On Dusseldorf; Elton John, Atlanta.
Nominated for *So Now Then* by Jon Bird, Professor of Art and Critical Theory at Middlesex University, UK.

MICHAEL WESELY, born Munich, Germany, 1963; studied at Bavarian State School for Photography, Munich (1986) and at the Academy of Fine Arts, Munich (1988–94). He currently lives and works in Berlin. He has exhibited widely, including solo shows at: Galeria Baro Cruz, São Paulo; Museum of Modern Art, New York; Fahnemann Projekte, Berlin; 25th São Paulo Biennale; Galleria Primo Piano, Rome; and Galeria Metta, Madrid. His work has been published several times, including: The Open Shutter Project, Museum of Modern Art, New York; and East Germany, Walther König Verlag, Cologne.
Nominated for *So Now Then* by Mathias Harder Curator, Helmut Newton Foundation, Berlin.

DAVID CAMPANY is a writer, artist and Reader in Photography at the University of Westminster. His essays have appeared in a number of exhibition catalogues and anthologies, including *Cruel and Tender: The Real in the Twentieth Century Photograph* (Tate, 2003), *Singular Images: Essays on Remarkable Photographs* (Tate, 2005) and *Rewriting Conceptual Art* (Reaktion, 1999). He has written for many journals including *Source*, *Art Review*, *Contemporary* and the *Oxford Art Journal*. His book *Art and Photography* was published in 2003 (Phaidon) and he is currently working on a book about dialogues between cinema and photography (Reaktion). His photographic project *Adventures in the Valley*, made in collaboration with Polly Braden, was shown at the Institute of Contemporary Arts, London, in 2005.

MARTHA LANGFORD is an Assistant Professor of Art History at Concordia University in Montreal. Founding Director/Chief Curator of the Canadian Museum of Contemporary Photography in Ottawa (1985–94), Langford received her Ph.D. from McGill University in 1997, followed by fellowships held at the Institute for the Humanities of Simon Fraser University and the National Gallery of Canada. Major works on photography include *Suspended Conversations: The Afterlife of Memory in Photographic Albums* (2001) and an edited collection, *Image & Imagination* (2005). Her forthcoming book is *Scissors, Paper, Stone: Expressions of Memory in Contemporary Photographic Art*. Her essays have appeared in numerous catalogues, journals, and edited collections; she has co-edited two special issues of journals: *West Coast Line* (2001) and *exposure* (1998). Langford is a contributing editor for *Border Crossings* (Winnipeg) and sits on the advisory panel of *BlackFlash* (Saskatoon). An active independent curator, she was Artistic Director of the international photographic biennale, Le Mois de la Photo à Montréal 2005.

JAN-ERIK LUNDSTRÖM is the Director of BildMuseet, Umeå University, Umeå, Sweden, a museum of contemporary art and visual culture. He is also active as a freelance curator, critic and cultural organizer. Among his latest exhibitions are *Politics of Place, Killing Me Softly* (Tirana Biennial), *Projects for a Revolution* (Mois de la Photo, Montreal), *Double Vision* (Prague Biennale) and *Same, Same, but Different*. He was the Chief Curator of Berlin Photography Festival, 2005, where he produced the exhibition *After the Fact*, a major survey of documentary practices in contemporary art. He is the author of numerous books, including *Nordic Landscapes, Tankar om fotografi* [Thoughts on Photography], *Irving Penn* and *Horizons: Towards a Global Africa*. He is a guest professor at HISK, Antwerp, Belgium and at the Kunstakademie, Oslo, Norway. Lundström is a prolific international lecturer and writer, contributor to symposia internationally and to cultural magazines such as *Glänta, European Photography*, *Paletten* and *tema celeste*.